EncourageMe-N-It

30-Day Devotional of
Encouragement & Reflection

By Natoshia D. Mayer

Copyright 2020 Natoshia D. Mayer

All rights reserved. No portion of this book may be reproduced in any form without permission from the publisher, except as permitted by U.S. Copyright law. The use of short quotations or occasional page copying for personal or group study is permitted and encouraged.

All Scripture quotations, unless otherwise indicated, are taken from the King James Version of the Holy Bible.

Printed in the United States of America

ISBN: 978-1-7353960-2-6

Published By: Janay Roberson
Awaken U Publishing Company
www.janayroberson.com

Contents

Dedication v

Foreword vi

1 Do Not Misread the Season 1

2 Betwixt My Past and My Promise 6

3 Unfinished 11

4 A Trip to the Master Restorer 15

5 See Me Now but Look at Me Later 20

6 My Womb Speaks for Me 25

7 I Am Ready to Walk Again 30

8 What Happens When I am Uzziah? 34

9 Beaten, Bruised, Bleeding, but Midnight Is on the Way
   39

10 Whatever It Takes, Get to the Shore! 43

11 I Had a Moment, but I Am Alright Now 47

12 Access Denied: It Is All About Access! 52

13 Flawed and Faithful 57

14 I Have Power Now but Wait Until I Die! 61

15 It Is My Shifting Season 65

16 I Made the Cut! 69

17 A Necessary Sacrifice 74

18 Pig Pen Revival.. 78

19 RSVP for the Marriage Supper of the Lamb 83

20 The Promise, the Instructions, the Manifestation 88

21 Who Is It?... 92

22 Where Is Your Faith?... 96

23 Birthing Promise 100

24 Three Strikes, You Are In!..................................... 106

25 You Took My Coat, But God Gave Me a Kingdom
    111

26 Course Shift Ahead 115

27 Hold On, Help Is on the Way! 120

28 Your Position Makes All Things Possible!............ 125

29 You Have Your Instructions, Now Go Win the Battle
    130

30 Press in, Pass By, and Touch 134

Dedication

This book is dedicated in memory to one of the greatest encouragers I know, my big brother, my hero, William E. Robinson.

(1969-2019)

Foreword

There are times when we as souls require both tending and mending. As believing sojourners who constantly live in the tension of being in the world yet not of it, the culmination of compassion and encouragement from others serves as a sorely needed balm, a soothing salve for the places, according to Philip Bennett, "where life has penetrated us."

This daily devotional that God has breathed within Natoshia D. Mayer to share with the world is a much needed reminder of what is "really real" about the narrow way leads to life-the consistent, countercultural walk with the Lord that is rewarding yet challenging. Therefore, encouragement in its truest essence is inspiration laced with hope and promise that what lies ahead is worth the struggle, and it is this very thing that Natoshia's words offer to all of us who have ears to hear what the Spirit of God is speaking.

Paulleatha Bruce, MDiv
Empowerment Coach and Counselor
The Uncommon Tapestry, LLC

1

Do Not Misread the Season

"Jesus said unto him, if thou canst believe, all things are possible to him that believeth"
(Mark 9:23).

Without fail, every year has four seasons, although some seasons may feel similar to others. Like natural seasons, spiritual seasons also change. We have all experienced difficult seasons in our Christian walk. We have had doubts and fears about fulfilling our purpose and destiny on the earth. We have questioned whether we will truly experience and embrace the full richness of life, as well as the joy and grace given by God. These doubts and fears are what I call symptoms of a season, indicators that further reading is necessary, and we should believe deeper.

The journey to all things being possible starts with belief. When our belief or faith is being attacked, the result is a misread season. It is a misread season because we may think and feel we are being punished for something we did or failed to do. Our brains do not automatically assume the best. Oftentimes, it assumes the worse, which leads to more doubts and fears.

When doctors cannot determine what is immediately wrong with a patient, they treat the symptoms. If after a period of time the symptoms do not improve, further testing is required. Spiritually, we can be guilty of reacting to or treating the symptoms only. We falsely determine the cause of what is wrong based on the symptoms. We treat what is seen. However, faith is unseen. Therefore, we need to dig deeper to determine what is actually happening. We need to learn to read our seasons.

Trouble and trial symptoms do not always indicate you are in a bad season. What seem to be unanswered prayers are not signs that God has abandoned you. These are all symptoms we experience at some point in our walk with Christ. We absolutely cannot judge or read our seasons based on them. Instead, we need to remember that symptoms have purpose. Trials and troubles come to give us strength, purify us, and draw us closer to God. They can also reveal deeper issues we need to deal with, which we may have buried and forgotten. Symptoms can include depression, anxiety, fear of failure, fear of success, and disbelief. The key is to treat these symptoms with the Word of God.

Symptoms can be treated by not putting much stock on the symptoms but the Savior. What does the Word say about overcoming doubt, fears, and disbelief?

We cannot allow our symptoms to make us misread the season. If you are struggling to believe what God has shown or promised you, look to His Word. If you are struggling to find yourself and your place in the world, look to His Word. Whatever you need is in the Word of God! Say to yourself, "My symptoms will not cause me to misread my season."

Just because you are having these symptoms does not mean God has changed His mind about what He is going to do for and through you. However, you must treat the symptoms of disbelief with the Word of God before you can receive. The presence of symptoms does not negate the blessings of the season.

When your symptoms become overwhelming, God is up to something. And where God is taking you, these symptoms cannot go. Read seasons and symptoms correctly. Read them as an indicator that something needs to happen before something happens. In other words, if I cannot walk in "all things are possible" until I believe, then I need to build my faith.

Read your season beyond your symptoms. Do not be afraid to dig deeper. Ask yourself why. Why am I being tested in this particular area at this particular time? For example, if your faith is being tried. Why is it being tried?

EncourageMe-N-It

This particular season you are in right now could be a faith-building season. You can choose to see it as negative or positive. If it is seen as negative, then the season is being misread. If it is seen as positive, it will be read as a season of patience building. Whatever your season may be, whatever you are facing in this season, know that all things work together for good!

It is the job of the Enemy to keep us distracted by making us focus on the symptoms. He makes us judge our seasons by our symptoms. But symptoms can be treated and once that is done, the only thing left to do is enjoy the season.

Do not despise the season you are in. Remember, every season has a purpose. Once you recognize the purpose, you will yield, not only a "reaping" result but also an "All things are possible" result.

"And let us not be weary in well doing: for in due season we shall reap if we faint not" (Galatians 6:9)

Reflection & Application Questions:

1. What symptoms in your life have led you to believe you are in a bad season?

2. Based on what you have read, how will you now see your current season?

Scriptures for Further Encouragement: James 1:2-4

2

Betwixt My Past and My Promise

"The Lord is not slack concerning his promise, as some men count slackness; but is longsuffering to us-ward, not willing that any should perish, but that all should come to repentance"
(2 Peter 3:9).

A betwixt and between season can be compared to that of the children of Israel coming out of Egypt. After God worked the miracles necessary to free them from bondage, the trip to the Promised Land ensued. At the exit, the children of Israel did not know the hard experiences of the in-between stage. They were ecstatic about their deliverance but unaware of what they were about to endure betwixt their past and their promise. If you know the story, you know they wandered in the betwixt for 40 years. As the journey got longer and longer, it was not the wilderness or the Red Sea that stood between the Israelites and their promise. It was what they did in the betwixt that delayed the promise. It was their murmuring and complaining. It was their lack of faith and distrust in the promises of God.

How many of us can say, "I know what God said! I believe what God said! But the season of betwixt and between can be a rough one"? It seems as if you will never receive the promise. May I submit to you, the rougher it is, the more faith you will need. The betwixt season requires your faith to be on full! You will know when you are there because though you are in the betwixt and between, you cannot be moved!

The wilderness is designed to show you and God (although He already knows) what is in you. The Israelites started the journey with praises but could not maintain them when their bellies got hungry. Their minds told them it was better in Egypt. Often, who you really are shows in the wilderness. However, the question is, can you believe God when you are betwixt your past and your promise? Can you believe God when your past is still close enough for you to see? When it seems as if your past is closer to you than your promise, can you trust God? Many times, the heat is turned up before freedom and your breakthrough comes.

You should look at the betwixt and between as an indication you are closer to your promise than your past. God is not a man that He should lie. If He said it, it will come to pass. If He made you a promise, it will be manifested. In times of betwixt and between, lean on your faith and trust in God. Regardless of how long it takes,

God's promise will be fulfilled because you trust and have faith in Him. Disbelief and disobedience added time in the wilderness for the Israelites. Do not let that be your testimony. What you do in the in-between and betwixt times determines how quickly you get to the promise. How you handle your wilderness determines how quickly you walk in the promise. Do not be a murmurer and complainer in the betwixt. But be a praiser! Stand on faith. Faith tells me that although I am closer to my past than my promise, I am moving. The more I move, the farther I am from my past, and the closer I am to my future. Do not faint in the betwixt season because you are on your way to promise!

Keep marching! Promise is coming into view. Keep trusting! Yes, it gets hard sometimes but continue to believe because nothing is too hard for God. Going back to what is comfortable will not work. Slavery is never better than freedom regardless of the trials and tribulations that come your way. Trust the process and before you know it, you will be in a land flowing with milk and honey.

What you do in the in-between times determines how quickly you will get to the promise. You may say, "My past is still close enough for me to see. Actually, it's closer to me than my promise." The same was true for Abraham but he trusted God. The same was true for David. He had enemies who wanted to see him dead, but he trusted God. And the same is true for you, regardless of your past, your promise stands sure. Trust God!

Handle delay well. "How we handle God's ordained delays is a good measure of our spiritual maturity. If we allow such delays to make us drift off into sin or lapse in resignation to fate, then we react poorly to His ordained delays. If we allow such times to deepen our perseverance in following God, then they are of good use" (*Enduring Word Bible Commentary*).

No matter the distance between our past and the promise, we will always get to the promise. The lessons in between strengthen us for the journey.

In pursuit of promise anything can happen!

Reflection & Application Questions:

1. What is about to die in you because you want to give up prematurely?

2. Based on what you have read, what will you change, learn, or strengthen to ensure you receive what God promised you?

Scripture for Further Encouragement: Galatians 6:9

3

Unfinished

"Beloved, now are we the sons of God, and it doth not yet appear what we shall be: but we know that, when he shall appear, we shall be like him; for we shall see him as he is"

(1 John 3:2).

The word "unfinished" has several definitions, including "not finished; not ended or to the desired final state; incomplete" (*Webster's Dictionary*).

I like to use 1 John 3:2 to shed some light on what I think about when I hear the word "unfinished" as it pertains to the body of Christ—you and me. This verse states, "Beloved, now are we the sons of God, and it doth not yet appear what we shall be: but we know that, when he shall appear, we shall be like him; for we shall see him as he is." Another applicable verse is Jeremiah 29:11, "For I know the thoughts that I think towards you, saith the Lord, thoughts of peace, and not evil, to give you an expected end." We may not be fully aware of our end but rest assured God is.

The journey from unfinished to finished is a process, which is not always pretty or easy, but it is necessary. Many things that are now beautiful and flawless were not so in their initial stages. Why? Because they were unfinished. In your raw stage, it does not yet appear what you shall be. Enduring the process will reveal what you really are.

I use two examples to describe the significance of the process: a diamond and an olive. Think of a diamond! In its raw state, it is not as shiny and flawless. Diamonds endure the process to get to their finished state. But after the process, they are beautiful and flawless. It is important to remember that even though a diamond's latter appearance is better than its former, the diamond is just as valuable at the raw stage. The point here is that **your unfinished stage does not define your finished stage. Who you are now is not necessarily who you will be at the end. Don't** devalue yourself because you are in the process. The process makes you flawless!

A different example of the process is the olive. Jekalyn Karr has a song that talks about the three stages an olive goes through. She says, "It has to go through the shaking, the beating, and the pressing for its oil to flow." Flowing oil is the result of a process. The processing of a diamond and an olive is different. Unlike the diamond, the olive is already what it shall be, or is it? If you look at an olive, you will see it is in its finished state until it is needed in a different capacity, thereby starting a new process!

Where are you at this point in life? Are you a diamond or an olive? Admittedly, sometimes we are both. I submit to you today that like the olive and the oil, it does not yet fully appear what we shall be. Why? Because we are simply unfinished.

Life shakes you up, beats you down, and presses into you so your oil can flow. Something good has started in you, and God will complete it. Endure the process. Parts and pieces of you have to be cut away because God is still working on you. You are not finished yet.

When God gets through with you, you shall come forth polished, flawless, and flowing! All while being confident of this very thing: He which hath begun a good work in you will perform it until the day of Jesus Christ (Philippians 1:6).

Reflection & Application Questions:

1. Where do you see yourself in the finishing process?

2. When reading Jeremiah 29:11, how does it speak to you?

3. Based on what you have read, what will you change, learn, or strengthen to ensure you endure the finishing process?

Scriptures for Further Encouragement: Isaiah 55:8-12, Hebrews 10:36, Romans 12:12

4

A Trip to the Master Restorer

"Restore unto me the joy of thy salvation; and uphold me with thy free spirit"
(Psalm 51:12).

Restoration is defined as bringing back something to a former position or condition.

Anything can be restored. Furniture, old cars, buildings, even hair can be restored. In addition to all these things, people can be restored. This text speaks of David's heart. David was known for being a man after God's own heart. However, that is not the only reason he is known. David was guilty of adultery and murder. He deserved death, but because he repented, God sent restoration. That being said, notice David's restoration came at the cost of his child. Sin always comes with a cost! And even though David fasted and prayed, the child was not spared. In his time of distress, David wrote Psalm 51.

EncourageMe-N-It

At some point in our lives, we will need restoration. Regardless of title or position, all of us will face that time when we have gone too far and said too much, times when we give out and give out until we are empty. At those times, we need to be restored. Maybe you did not commit adultery or kill, but you said something hurtful to someone. Maybe you joked one time too many. Maybe you said something about someone and word got back to the person. Now, you are guilty of an offense. You hurt someone emotionally. But God restored you instead of condemning you. Yes, you must deal with the consequences of your actions, but God will bring life back to you.

At the point of his sin, David lost his joy! But at the point of repentance, God restored his joy! Thank God for being a restorer and a forgiving God.

The natural restoration process is interesting and relatable to the spiritual restoration process. When something needs to be restored in the natural, you must take it to a person who specializes in restoration. If you take it to the wrong person, he will make it worse or worthless. Therefore, you must take it to a professional restorer. There are two examples of restoration that I have observed: a good cleaning and stripping away.

1. A Good Cleaning

David went to the Professional Restorer because he needed a good cleaning! He said to the professional restorer:

"Wash me thoroughly from mine iniquity, and cleanse me from my sin. 7. Purge me with hyssop, and I shall be clean: wash me, and I shall be whiter than snow" (Psalm 51:2).

2. Stripping Away

Some of us may need this other kind of restoration. Maybe you messed up badly like David. Maybe your situation requires a little more work in addition to washing. There is a process in furniture restoration where there must first be a stripping away of the old to make room for the new. The more layers, the more stripping is needed. After the stripping is complete, cracks and broken places are fixed and holes filled in. The last step is to apply stain and the piece is fully restored.

Sometimes we need to be stripped of old stuff because there are layers and layers and layers of old junk in our lives. The old needs to be stripped away and replaced with the new. Holes were left in your heart by folks who hurt you. Those holes need to be filled in by the love of Christ. Perhaps you have been cracked because someone mishandled and dropped you. You never got over it. You just kept covering it with stain. Are you covered by layers and layers of hurt? The Master Restorer I talked about earlier also specializes in strip restoration. He can strip your life of anything that is damaging you. He can fix what is cracked and fill in the holes with more of Himself. He will strip off years of pain, guilt, and sin and then apply the blood-stained banner to your life.

When He is finished, you will come forth healed, whole, and shining as pure gold. Some may say you cannot be fixed; you are too damaged, or you are too far gone. I say this Master Restorer can fix anybody who has been anywhere, doing everything, no matter how long. All it takes is for you to open your mouth like David; acknowledge your need and ask for the Master Restorer. The Master Restorer will step in and take it from there.

"But what saith it? The word is nigh thee, even in thy mouth, and in thy heart: that is, the word of faith, which we preach; That if thou shalt confess with thy mouth the Lord Jesus, and shalt believe in thine heart that God hath raised him from the dead, thou shalt be saved" (Romans 10:8-9, KJV).

Reflection & Application Questions:

1. Think back over your life. Have you ever experienced a time when you failed miserably and thought God would not forgive you? How did you feel when you learned forgiveness was possible and provided?

2. Based on what you have read, what will you change, learn, or strengthen to ensure you know no matter how bad a situation, God is a restorer?

Scripture for Further Encouragement: Psalm 103:8-12

5

See Me Now but Look at Me Later

"Then Peter said, Silver and gold have I none; but such as I have give I thee: In the name of Jesus Christ of Nazareth rise up and walk"

(Acts 3:6).

The word "see" is defined as to perceive by the eye. The word "look" is defined as to expect, anticipate; to have in mind as an end.

In Acts Chapter 3, Peter and John went up to the temple to pray. There, a man who was lame from his mother's womb sat at the temple gate. Daily, this man was carried to the gate to beg for alms. At the hour of prayer, Peter and John came to the temple to pray and the man asked alms of them. Peter and John said, "Look on us!" The man gave heed to them *expecting* to receive something from them. However, Peter said, "Silver and gold have I none but such as I have, I give to you. In the name of Jesus Christ rise up and walk" (verse 6). They took him by the hand, lifted him up, and his bones gained strength to stand. In response to the *look* were *expectation* and *anticipation*. However, instead of giving the man silver or gold, Peter and John gave him something even better. They gave him healing.

Is it possible we have not received because what we asked for is not as important as what we can have? Having silver and gold was important for this man but the ability to walk was even more important. Raise your expectations!

Healing was the result of a *look*. Next, is the response of the *see*. The people saw the man jumping and praising God and knew him as the lame beggar at the temple. Consequently, they wondered and were amazed at what happened.

I encourage you to *look*. Expect, anticipate, and have an end goal in mind. Right now, people may *see* you and underestimate you based on your appearance as they did the lame man. Or they may look at you and see a walking cane or tears flowing down your face. They may *see* you in one of the greatest battles of your life. They may even *see* you in the "barely making ends meet" season. This is because they are at "see," not at "look." Someone needs to hear you say, "See me now, but look at me later!"

Jesus the Christ, Son of the Living God, aka the "such as I have" is going to do something so great and miraculous in your life that your perception will be your reality. And it is not going to be accomplished by silver and gold. It is going to be accomplished by your *look*—by your expectation, anticipation, and having in mind what your end will be. Do you already have in mind what you want the Lord to do for you?

Based on what God will do for me, I would much rather be looked at than seen. Our now season requires a *see*. Our next season requires a *look*! And once God does it in us, then comes the *see* from others. They will *see* and be amazed. Why? Because the last time they saw you, you were a spiritually lame beggar. Now, you have been lifted and strengthened. Now you are leaping, jumping, and praising God.

Do not judge yourself or others in their "see" season because that is only a perception. If you only see me, you are making a predetermination of what and who I am by what you see. You are perceiving with the natural eye. I want you to see me after my "look" season.

In my look season, I have expected; I have anticipated, and I have received my miracle!

That is why we praise God as if we have no sense. That is why we will never doubt God regardless of what season we are in. We know in spite of it all, the "such as I have" is ready, willing, and able to come and see about you!

You know that "Eye hath not seen, nor ear heard, neither have entered into the heart of man, the things which God hath prepared for them that love him" (1 Corinthians 2:9).

Natoshia D. Mayer

What God has in store for you and me cannot be seen, heard, or felt. It can only be experienced! So be encouraged. Things may not look the way you want them to but keep on looking. Keep on expecting. Sooner or later, you will look like what you are! Sooner or later, people will see what God has done in your life. They may even have to look twice because you will no longer look like what you were. I encourage you to look again!

Reflection & Application Questions:

1. Think back over your life. Have you ever experienced a time when you were discouraged based on what you saw (perceived)?

2. Based on what you have read, what will you change, learn, or strengthen to ensure you know no matter what it looks like, no matter what you see, you will always trust God to change your perception?

Scripture for Further Study and Encouragement: Jeremiah 29:11, 1 Peter 5:7

6

My Womb Speaks for Me

"Wherefore it came to pass, when the time was come about after Hannah had conceived, that she bare a son, and called his name Samuel, saying, Because I have asked him of the Lord"
(1 Samuel 1:20).

Womb – A place where something is developing

The biblical story of Hannah is well-known. Hannah, a baroness, was tormented by Peninnah the second wife of her husband because she was barren. The Bible says that Peninnah provoked Hannah sore to make her fret because the Lord shut up Hannah's womb. Elkanah, Hannah's husband loved her dearly and yearly gave her a worthy portion. But this particular time when the family took the yearly trip to the temple to offer sacrifices, Hannah poured her heart out to God. Eli, the priest, thought Hannah was drunk. What he witnessed was a woman full of sorrow who moved her lips but no sound came forth. Seeing how sorrowful Hannah was, Eli told her that the Lord would grant her petition.

We can gain encouragement from this story in knowing that though all battles require fighting, you are just not the one who fights in all of them. Some are won by production. What God has ordained for you to produce is being developed in your womb. Other people may produce before you and may even produce more than you. However, God will do for you what He did for Hannah. What God did for Hannah, people will continue to read about for the rest of time. Notice that not once are the children of the provoker (Peninnah) listed by name. In this instance, Hannah's womb spoke for her. She did not have to address her adversary, her tormentor. Her womb did the talking for her.

So when you look at your life and think, "Why am I not producing?" and "Why am I not further along in life by now?" God is developing something in you that has the potential to change history. You are not running behind. Just because it may take a little longer for you, does not mean your baby will not come. Quality is better than quantity on any day.

Hannah was not just producing a son; she was producing a prophet. Anybody can have a child, but not everybody can have a prophet! A prophet who will serve the very first king of Israel. A prophet who will go and find a shepherd boy by the name of David and anoint him the second king of Israel. This same David's lineage birthed the Savior of the world—Jesus the Christ, Son of the Living God.

So, do not worry when it seems you should be further along in life by now, when it seems you should be operating with precision in your gift and calling by now. Do not worry when it seems everybody is out-running you in ministry. Keep your pace and trust God. After all, the Bible said God shut up Hannah's womb! So if He shut it, He can open it!

In this season, do not worry about using your mouth to get back at those Peninnah's on the earth, those who laugh, point fingers, and talk about you. This battle does not require words. What others do is not your focus. Sooner or later, your womb will speak for you! Your vision may be tarrying longer than you want it to, but one day, it will not tarry; it will come to pass. Do not get weary in waiting.

My baby—my gift, my calling, my assignment, may be taking a while for me to master, but it only has until the end of the last trimester. At that time, ready or not, it will come forth speaking! And everyone will know this was the work of the Lord. Say to your womb, "Speak womb speak!"

Can you believe God that something is being developed in you and on your behalf? It is already in you! You already have what it takes. It just needs to be developed, grown, and then birthed. What are you birthing? Essentially life—life that has the ability to give life is growing inside of you. You have the ability to sustain life! A gift and calling are growing and developing inside of you. Whether it takes nine months or nine years, when it comes forth, it will come forth speaking! Why? Because you did what you were supposed to do. You prayed; you believed the Word, and you acted on the Word. Now, your womb can produce. Your womb can speak for you. And all of your naysayers can only watch you produce.

Say what you want about your delayed production; this situation does not require your words. It is not even about you; it is about what God will produce through you as a result of your faith and trust in Him. He will get the glory out of your life.

In this season of birthing, do not use your words. Do not say everything you want or are going to do. Do not broadcast everything God is saying to you. Some Peninnah's out there think it is all about them. They think they are the only ones making things happen. Again, your womb will speak for you. When it speaks, it will be so loud and clear, it will silence the mouth of your tormentor. Believe the Word of God.

Reflection & Application Questions:

1. Think back over your life. Have you ever used words to fight your battles? How did you feel afterward? Was it as satisfying as you thought it would be?

2. Based on what you have read, what will you change, learn, or strengthen to avoid responding to naysayers? Will you allow your womb to speak for you?

Scripture for Further Encouragement: 1 Samuel Chapter 1

7

I Am Ready to Walk Again

"And when they could not find by what way they might bring him in because of the multitude, they went upon the housetop, and let him down through the tiling with his couch into the midst before Jesus"
(Luke 5:19).

This biblical account is about a paralyzed man who had friends full of faith. These friends had heard of Jesus' miracles and hoped their friend could experience the same. Upon arrival, the men could not get to Jesus because people had come from all over the place to witness miracles and to hear Him teach. Because of the crowd, an alternative route had to be sought. The men took the stairs to the roof. There, they began to tear up and break down the obstacles and barriers in their way, so they could get to Jesus. Once they got the man to Jesus, the man was healed and able to walk again.

Our greatest blessings, healing, deliverance, and miracles always obstacles or barriers in front of them. How we handle our obstacles and barriers determines when we get to our blessings. Barriers literally block entrances, so you cannot get through, for example, the concrete blocks highway workers use on the highway. These barriers are there to divert traffic.

The Enemy uses barriers and obstacles to divert you from your destined place. They are there for no other reason than to get you to go back because you cannot see your way around them. But if you go back because of obstacles and barriers, you will never walk. However, if you are determined that not one obstacle or barrier will stop you from walking again, you will find another way. You will take another route because you are determined to walk again.

Whether obstacle or barrier, both must be overcome before healing can take place. What is it in your life that needs to be overcome before you can walk again? Obstacles and barriers come like clockwork at times. When you get through one thing, here comes another. And at some point in your journey, you may get tired and say, "It is what it is. I will never better my condition. This is just the hand that I was dealt, so I will just be satisfied in my state of lack and not having enough!"

It is great to find some good friends to take the roof off for you when you can't. These friends say, "Yes, we see the barriers and obstacles, so what?" We all need friends who will go the distance for us just as we will for them, friends who do not just want to be in one-sided friendships getting all the benefits and not giving. You need friends who will not allow you to sit around in a stinking thinking tank. Rather, they will say, "Yes, they did you wrong, but you will not sit here in this pit. We will find a way to get you where you need to be, so you can reach your destiny."

Good friends will say, "I know you are crying but dry those tears. No ma'am, no sir, you will not die in this lame place. No matter what we have to do, you will be successful. Even if it must come out of our pockets, you will be successful!" Who would not want friends like this? This man's friends tore the roof off someone else's house because they wanted their friend healed.

When you do not feel like praying or seeking God, find friends who will lift you in the spirit, as well as tear down obstacles in the way to get you to Jesus. By any means necessary, they will get you to the place where you are ready to walk again.

Say to yourself, "I need to walk again! It is crucial that I walk again! Life has handed me some serious obstacles and barriers that knocked me down onto my sick bed. But today, I want to take up my bed and walk. I am ready to walk again! And this time, when I walk again, I will be careful to protect my walk, so I will never have to be carried again.

Reflection & Application Questions:

1. What are the main barriers and obstacles keeping you from walking at this point in your life?

2. Based on what you have read, what will you change, learn, or strengthen to overcome obstacles and take up your spiritual bed and walk?

Scriptures for Further Encouragement: Romans 5:3-5

8

What Happens When I am Uzziah?

"In the year that king Uzziah died I saw also the Lord sitting upon a throne, high and lifted up, and his train filled the temple"
(Isaiah 6:1).

King Uzziah was initially a great king. He became the king at the age of 16 and reigned for 52 years. He was known for restoring Judah and doing what was right in the eyes of God. He had a great resume, which included defeating the Philistines, breaking down walls, rebuilding cities, digging wells, and having a well-trained army. King Uzziah was famous far and near. However, he became prideful in his accomplishments and power. Pride always goes before destruction. Because the king knew how powerful and famous he was, he took it upon himself to participate in incense burning, which was reserved only for the priest. When the priest tried to stop him, he became angry. The Bible teaches the king was angry and as he yelled at the priest, leprosy appeared on his forehead. He was rushed out of the temple and lived in isolation with leprosy until the day he died.

So the question is what happens when I am Uzziah? What happens when pride displaces you from your original focus on God? If we are not careful, our pride will make us attempt to lift ourselves where only God can lift us because we think we can go there.

You are prospering; your name is being spread on the earth; you are building and doing your thing. But because you took it upon yourself to touch what you were not ordained to touch, it will lead you to isolation and death.

Significantly, the king's death allowed someone else to see the Lord. Isaiah did not see the Lord until King Uzziah died. The Bible does not describe the relationship Isaiah had with Uzziah. It just lets us know that when Uzziah died, Isaiah saw the Lord. What aspect of Uzziah needs to die for you to see the Lord? Where is the source of our pride? Do we take the credit for what we have and where we are? Isaiah said: "In the year King Uzziah died I saw the Lord." Some of us need to say: "In the year I died, I saw the Lord."

Seeing the Lord requires self-examination. Once His presence shows up, you will see yourself just as you are. Isaiah saw himself once the other stuff was removed. He said, "Woe is me!" He called himself undone with unclean lips in the midst of people with unclean lips.

EncourageMe-N-It

We are good at seeing everyone else's sins, but what about our own? Can we see where we fell short and allowed pride to creep in?

"Woe is me! for I am undone; because I am a man of unclean lips, and I dwell in the midst of a people of unclean lips: for mine eyes have seen the King, the Lord of hosts" (Isaiah 6:5).

God's presence is like a mirror that causes you to see you!

That is why we need the presence of God.

That is why we cannot just come to church and go through the motions!

No, we need God's presence to show up.

His presence shines the light in your closet.

His presence comes revealing you to you!

Can we admit there were times in our lives when we were undone and had unclean lips? I have been to some places and said some things—but God! Can we honestly say, "I have been Uzziah! But Uzziah has to die! Pride has to die!"?

We need God to touch our lips with live coal from the altar and purge our sins away.

David said, "Purge me with hyssop and I shall be clean; wash me and I shall be whiter than snow" (Psalm 51:7). Once this happens, you will be like Isaiah when God asks whom He shall send and who will go? You can say, "Here am I, Lord, send me!" Why? Because now I am washed, clean, and ready for service. The elements of Uzziah are no longer stopping me from seeing You. I am ready to do what You have called me to do. I am ready to be that person You use to accomplish Your will on the earth! Like Isaiah said, "Here am I; send me."

Questions

1. Was there ever a time in your life when you struggled with pride? How did you handle it?

2. Based on what you have read, what will you change, learn, or strengthen to ensure you keep pride in check and be fit for sending?

Scripture for Further Encouragement: 2 Chronicles Chapter 26; Isaiah Chapter 6

9

Beaten, Bruised, Bleeding, but Midnight Is on the Way

"And at midnight Paul and Silas prayed, and sang praises unto God: and the prisoners heard them. And suddenly there was a great earthquake, so that the foundations of the prison were shaken: and immediately all the doors were opened, and every one's bands were loosed"
(Acts 16:25-26).

Midnight signifies a transition of time from one to the next. There are several biblical occurrences of things happening at midnight—from prayer to death. In this particular passage, prayer and praise brought deliverance. Paul and Silas were thrown into jail for casting the Devil out of a woman following them. Because this lady's boss got upset about the loss of income, he had them thrown into jail. They were beaten, bruised, and bleeding. However, at midnight, Paul and Silas prayed and sang praises! They sang and prayed so loudly all the prisoners heard them. And then, they received one of those "suddenly, at once" miracles. A rumbling began and along came a great earthquake that shook the foundations of the prison. Then immediately, all the doors were opened, and everyone's bands were loosed.

Honestly, when we are cut and bleeding, our first action or thought is not to hold a praise and worship service. Most of the time, we feel we have done something wrong. Let us re-train our brains away from thinking trouble is the result of something we have done wrong. We can learn some important lessons from this story. First, sometimes doing the right thing gets you into trouble.

Sooner or later, you will come to expect that the Devil will try something. You will realize you always need to be prayed and praised up. In good times, pray. In bad times, pray. Remember we ought to always pray and not faint (Luke 18:1). In good times, praise and in bad times, praise. You might be beaten, bruised, and bleeding, but midnight is on the way.

I hear that midnight is the darkest hour of the day. Just when it seems darkest in your life, God will move on your behalf. Your job is to pray and praise. The Bible says "I will bless the Lord at all times. His praise shall continually be in my mouth" (Psalm 34:1). Therefore, I will give Him praise. It does not matter what it looks like. It does not matter what it feels like, it does not even matter what it is. I am going to praise Him. Why? Because He is worthy regardless of what I am going through. He is God and besides Him, there is no other. He has all power in His hand. He promised to deliver me out of all my troubles. And I know if I call on the Lord, He will come and see about His child. He may not come when we want Him to come, but He is always on time. Yes, He is! Oh yes, He is. That is why I am going to praise Him.

I will take this beating because I know midnight is on the way. I will take this bruising because I know midnight is on the way. And I will take this bleeding because I know there is power in the blood of Jesus! I will open my mouth and sing praises unto His name. The more I praise Him, the more the ground of my trouble will shake. The more I pray, the more my problems will crumble. Then after a while when midnight comes, here comes my full-blown earthquake, my freedom! My bands will be loosed. Your bands will be loosed, and we will go forth from this prison with victory. Nothing by any means will stop me!

The Bible says in due season, we will reap if we faint not. That is why I will bless the Lord at all times. We praise a lot of people. Let us try praising God. For it is in Him we live and move and have our being. I praise Him because I cannot do anything without Him. Praise confuses the Enemy.

What can we learn from this story?

1. Sometimes doing the right thing gets you into trouble, but it is okay.

2. Regardless of what situation you are in, pray and praise anyway.

3. When you pray and praise, not only will your bands be loosed but so will the bands of everyone around you.

4. If you are beaten, bruised, and bleeding, hold on because midnight is on the way.

Scriptures for Further Encouragement: Psalm 119:62

10

Whatever It Takes, Get to the Shore!

"But the centurion, willing to save Paul, kept them from their purpose; and commanded that they which could swim should cast themselves first into the sea, and get to land: And the rest, some on boards, and some on broken pieces of the ship. And so it came to pass, that they escaped all safe to land"
(Acts 27:43-44).

After Saul was converted to Paul, some simply wanted him dead. Saul's past as a murderer of Christians meant he had to suffer a great deal. Some vowed they would not eat or drink until Paul was dead. Paul endured a great deal and was imprisoned. While on a ship to stand before Caesar, a storm arose. Although Paul warned that trouble was coming and the ship would not make it through, his warning was not heeded. And because they did not listen, they found themselves shipwrecked. When the storm did hit, Paul spoke up and told them they should have listened

EncourageMe-N-It

to him but also assured them everyone would survive, but the thing carrying them would not.

Far too long, we have been dependent on things/people who cannot carry us to our next place in God. But just like God destroyed the ship, He will destroy or remove your crutch. What happens when your job is gone, your family circle is broken, you lose your best friend, man, or your very support system? What then? Do you quit? Do you throw in the towel? Do you worry yourself sick? I encourage you to grab a broken piece and hold on. Because whatever happens, whatever you lose, whatever God takes away from you, you have to get to the shore.

When the ship had broken apart, the Bible says some came to shore on boards and some on broken pieces, but they all made it in. That means enough of the broken pieces were left **only** to get them to the shore, no further. Once they reached the shore, the broken pieces would have served their purpose. In other words, people have taken you as far as they can; it is up to God to take you further. Some people are like broken pieces; if you hold on to a broken piece too long, you will both go down. Do not be afraid to let go of broken pieces (people) who will cause you to sink. God will send others to bless you.

Other folks are on the shore waiting to bless you and restore all you had to unload to get to this place. Do not worry about what you had to give up because something more is waiting for you on the shore. What you gave up might have seemed important to you, but when the storm came it could not support or keep you safe. What you are about to receive will blow your mind! We serve a God of exceeding, abundantly, above all we ask or think blessings. Why worry about losing your security blanket when God is trying to give you a California king-sized comforter?

Whatever broken pieces of your life you need to get you to a safe place, use them. But only do so to get you there. Use them to get you to a place of blessings. Use them to get you to a place where God will show your enemies He is with you. No bite will harm you. As a matter of fact, you will shake off the vipers as Paul did. And when folks expect you to die, you will proclaim, "I shall live and not die!" You will come through without any swelling. That is the kind of God we serve.

Reflection & Application Questions:

1. How can you use the broken pieces in your life to get you to a place of safety in God?

2. Based on what you have read, what will you change, learn, or strengthen to ensure you get to a place of safety in God knowing He will take care of you?

Scriptures for Further Encouragement: Galatians 6:9, Proverbs 18:10

11

I Had a Moment, but I Am Alright Now

"And Ahab told Jezebel all that Elijah had done, and withal how he had slain all the prophets with the sword. Then Jezebel sent a messenger unto Elijah, saying, So let the gods do to me, and more also, if I make not thy life as the life of one of them by to morrow about this time"
(I Kings 19:1-2).

Elijah is no stranger to anyone who has been in church for any period of time. He was a prophet and God worked miracles through him. He lived in Israel during the reign of King Ahab and Jezebel. He was born a Tishbite and was nicknamed the "Troubler of Israel." Even with all that Elijah did for God, at this point in his life, he had a weak moment. He was down and depressed, hiding in a cave because of the wicked Jezebel.

So why was such a powerful man hiding in a cave? Before this moment, Elijah had caused the heavens to shut up, causing a drought for three years. He had multiplied flour and oil for a widow and her son. He later raised the widow's son from the dead. He also defeated 450 prophets of Baal with fire from heaven. After this event, word got back to the wicked queen Jezebel, and she was told what happened. She was furious with Elijah and said, "By this time tomorrow, I will make your life as the life of one of the dead prophets."

This is when Elijah had a weak moment. Elijah ran for his life. He fled to the wilderness, sat down under a tree, and requested that he should die. In response, Jesus asked Elijah, "What are you doing here?" And Elijah said he was jealous for God because the children of Israel had forsaken or gone away from God's covenant. He said they had thrown down the altars and killed the prophets. He was the only one left, and they wanted him dead, too.

The Enemy loves to make us think we are alone and no one understands what we are going through. No one sees what I am going through. My situation is so messed up. Everybody else is being blessed and prospering while I struggle every day.

God did not respond to Elijah's excuses. Instead, Elijah was told to go and stand on the mountain before the Lord and the Lord was going to pass by. The Lord passed by and a great and strong wind rent the mountains and broke into pieces the rocks before the Lord. But God was not in the wind. And after the wind an earthquake, but the Lord was not in the earthquake. And after the earthquake fire, but the Lord was not in the fire. And after the fire a still, small voice.

In our times of trials and tribulations, we experience weak moments. In those times, we look for God to move mightily. We look for grandiose signs of God coming to rescue us. We look for Him in the wind, earthquake, and fire. We want Him to move heaven and earth on our behalf, and sometimes He will. However, sometimes He comes in a still small voice, and we miss it because we want the big, miracle-working God.

What if He decides to get into the fire with you instead of removing the fire? We cannot dictate how God will deliver us. We need to know and believe that in due season, God will come down and see about His children. And if trouble is an indication of anything in this text, it is that a personal encounter with God is preceded by trouble.

Our job is to be still and know that God is God. He is well able to deliver us even in our weak moments. You may not even be standing in full strength right now. But do not be deceived. His strength is made perfect in your weakness. When you are weak, He is strong. And not only *when* you are weak, but *while* you are weak!

On your weakest day, remember the Devil is no match for the One fighting for you. I had a moment, but I am alright now. Everyone cannot bounce back from a moment but be determined that you will. Some cannot handle the manifold temptations. Think it not strange the fiery trails that try us (1 Peter 4:12). We must rejoice because we are partakers of Christ's sufferings. When His glory is revealed, we will be glad also.

Yes, it was strange that Elijah had a moment after he had slain all the prophets of Jezebel by calling fire down from heaven. This was his moment of weakness. What was yours? I am so glad God is not like man. No matter where you go and hide, God will chase you down. In Elijah's moment of weakness, God did not cut him off. Instead, He asked him a question. He said what are you doing here?

There are a couple of times in our walk when the Enemy fights us the hardest:
- After a great victory
- Before a great victory

Where are you right now? Are you at the end of a great victory? Or are you about to experience a great victory?

Elijah performed four more miracles after he had his moment:
1. Brought an end to the drought
2. Destroyed 51 soldiers with fire
3. Destroyed another 51 soldiers with fire
4. Parted the waters of the Jordan River

Now that you have had your weak moment, what miracles will God work through you?

Reflection & Application Questions:

1. Was there ever a time in your life when you had a weak moment, a loss of faith?

2. How did you overcome that moment?

3. Based on what you have read, what will you change, learn, or strengthen to ensure even when you have weak moments, they will not stop you?

Scripture for Further Encouragement and Study: 2 Corinthians 12:9

12

Access Denied: It Is All About Access!

"The thief cometh not, but for to steal, and to kill, and to destroy: I am come that they might have life, and that they might have it more abundantly"
(John 10:10).

Access is defined as permission, liberty, or ability to enter, approach, or pass to and from a place or to approach or communicate with a person or thing. Another definition is a means of approaching or entering a place.

John 10:10 teaches us that the Enemy desires to have access so he can steal, kill, and destroy. But the Enemy can only access the areas you have granted him permission to enter. Remember the definition of access: permission, liberty, or ability to enter approach or pass to and from. The key word in this definition is "permission."

So, if the Enemy comes to kill, steal, and destroy, he needs access through a vehicle that will get him to the thing or things he wants to kill, steal, or destroy. Some of his vehicles are unforgiveness, doubt/unbelief, fear, and double-mindedness.

To prevent or prohibit the Enemy from gaining access, we must learn to say, "Access denied!" Mark your territory. Let the Enemy know this is off-limits. Then you need to name your "this." Whatever your "this" is, let the Devil know access is denied.

Some of us gave access to things and people in the past that we need to give the pink slip to in this season. Why? They did not appreciate us. They were not real friends. Truth be told, they were enemies on assignment. That is called "Granted Access."

Admittedly, we have all granted access to folks who did not deserve it and those who mistreated it. For far too long, we have been trying to drag folks along who do not want to go anywhere. Furthermore, they are not concerned about you or your well-being.

From now on, pull over to the curb and let those folks out. You do not have time for that mess. Take back your "Access Granted" card. Those unworthy of your time should no longer have access to your time or attention. These folks need what I call "Blocked Access." It is like when you try to log on to something and forget your code. The system will give you at least three good tries to get in. After the third try and the code is still incorrect, you will be locked out of the system. Some of you have given folks more than three good tries; it is now time to lock them out of your system.

If you are not strong enough to do it, get some *access blockers*. Access blockers do exactly what their name is; they block access. Now, these are real friends. These are folks who have your back. You need to surround yourself with people who can see spiritually and have the Holy Ghost power. When the Enemy tries to come at you with one thing, your access blockers will say, "Not this time! You will not enter and wreak havoc on their lives. You are a liar and the truth is not in you!" Everybody needs a good access blocker. We all need people who can see the Enemy coming and block him. We have given too much access to the wrong people.

Your access to God is personal! It is not through the praises of others. It is through your personal praises. This is *personal access*. The Devil uses vehicles to kill, steal, and destroy. However, I will use the vehicle of personal praise to get to God.

I know what God did for me. I know how He brought me out and what He brought me out of. This is my "When I think of the goodness of Jesus, and all He has done for me" praise. This is my, "I know I did not deserve what He gave me access to, but He gave it to me anyway" praise. This is my "I owe Him" praise! That praise cannot come from you because you do not know God's goodness to me the way I do. You cannot tell it as I can tell it. You may not praise

Him adequately for the great things He has done for me. Therefore, I must give Him personal praise. This is my access praise.

The more I praise Him, the more I have access to Him. The more I praise Him, the more doors will begin to open. The more I praise Him, the more shackles and chains will break off me. The more I praise Him, the more victory I shall have. The more I praise Him, the more I can decree and declare what shall be in my life.

Because I praised Him in the low points of life, in the dry seasons, I now have access to the mountain top. I have been granted permission and liberty, as well as the ability to approach and enter His presence. I have heard that in His presence is the fullness of joy. In His presence is access.

Reflection & Application Questions:

1. Can you remember a time in your life when you gave the Enemy, someone, or something too much access?

2. What was the result of that access?

3. Based on what you have read, what will you change, learn, or strengthen to limit the access of the Enemy and strengthen your access to and from God?

Scriptures for Further Encouragement and Study: James 4:7

13

Flawed and Faithful

"If we confess our sins, he is faithful and just and will forgive us our sins and purify us from all unrighteousness"
(I John 1:9).

During his kingship, David made many mistakes. He was a murderer and an adulterer. True, he was flawed to the highest degree. Yet, God called him a man after His own heart. God does not discard us because we are flawed. He knows that without Him, we would utterly fall.

Cracked people still have value. God wants people who may be cracked but can still hold some water. You may be chipped. There may be a crack down the middle, but you can still hold the water. Imagine a mug with a broken handle. The handle is broken because life happened. Maybe it was dropped or abused, but it will still hold the water. It can still do what it was designed to do. The fact that the handle is broken does not mean it has to be thrown away. Likewise, you may be broken, but it does not mean God cannot pour life into you. Yes, life happened. Yes, you may have been dropped and broken. You may have been abused and misused, but you can still hold water. You can still do what you were created to do.

The key is to keep learning and growing even if you are flawed. Be determined even if you must walk in life with a limp. You are going forward. If you have to walk with a broken heart, press on! You may have been lied on and talked about but take the next step. You may have been dropped, but get up and keep walking, abused and misused, but you will not stop. Yes, you have flaws, but you are still moving on. You have flaws but you will remain faithful to the Lord. You are fragile, but God can still use you for the purpose you were created. You can still be used to carry out God's calling on your life. You can still be used to reach others who are broken, lost, and in need of a Savior. We were created to praise and magnify God. That does not require perfection; that requires faithfulness.

If brokenness is an indication that God will use you, then be encouraged to know God is not intimidated by your brokenness. He wants to heal your brokenness. He wants to take those flaws, buff them, and smoothen the rough edges. He wants you to shine like the sun. However, do not wait until you are perfectly restored. Let the Lord use you in your flawed stage. His strength is made perfect in your weakness. Today, I encourage you to understand you may be flawed, but in it all, remain faithful.

Reflection & Application Questions:

1. Have you ever felt God could not use you because all you could see were your imperfections?

2. Based on what you have read, what will you change, learn, or strengthen to stay encouraged and know that God is not looking for perfection, He is after faithfulness?

Scriptures for Further Encouragement and Study: Romans 5:8, James 3:2

14

I Have Power Now but Wait Until I Die!

"And when Jesus had cried with a loud voice, he said, Father, into thy hands I commend my spirit: and having said thus, he gave up the ghost"
(Luke 23:46).

Jesus had power even on the cross. He could have called for a legion of angels to come to His rescue, but He did not. His purpose was yet to be fulfilled. In order for something to live, something must first die. For us to have life and have it more abundantly, Jesus had to die.

At the point of crucifixion, many of us give up. We quit when times get tough. We give up when we have to go through pain and suffering, when trials and tribulations come back to back and there is no time to recover from the last storm. However, I encourage you not to quit because your purpose has not yet been fulfilled. In times like this, we seldom remember the power we have. Do not fool yourself; even in the midst of your tears, your body wrenching in pain, depression, and sad moments, you are powerful!

Yes, I have power now, but wait until I die! The point of spiritual crucifixion is for you to die to the flesh. Some are so scared to die because they cannot quite conceptualize the power we have after death. That power is different from the power we have now.

What do you mean Pastor Tot? What happens when you pass all of the tests and all of the assessments of one grade? You are promoted to the next grade. Well, you cannot get promoted until you die—not a physical death but your fleshly man must die. To get to the next level in God, you must pass every test and assessment on this level.

I do not know about you, but I sense at this time in human history, something great is about to break out. The warfare is intense, but the goal is to pass the test and prepare for our promotion to the next level. When you have been mocked, beaten, bruised, and nailed to the cross, you qualify for next-level power! That is why we should not always ask God to come in and take us out of what we are going through. Purpose and power are in that storm.

The Enemy desires to keep you in a tomb with a stone rolled in front. But just as he could not keep our Savior down, he cannot keep you down. He has a track record of trying but failing. So better yet, I can say with absolute certainty anything the Devil tries, will not work. With confidence, you can proclaim, "The Devil tried it, but he failed. The Devil is trying it, but he is failing. The Devil will try it, but he will fail.

Today, I encourage you not to be afraid to crucify your flesh. The resulting power is out of this world.

Reflection & Application Questions:

1. Taming the flesh is a constant task. How can you see beyond trials and tribulations to know they yield a greater anointing and power?

2. Based on what you have read, what will you change, learn, or strengthen to ensure you overcome the flesh and realize the power of God in your life?

Scripture for Further Encouragement and Study. Luke Chapter 24

15

It Is My Shifting Season

"And there were four leprous men at the entering in of the gate: and they said one to another, why sit we here until we die?"

(2 Kings 7:3).

Webster's Dictionary defines shift as "to change the place, position, or direction of: move."

A shift requires movement. Before the Prodigal Son went from a place of lack to a place of more, he had to get up from the pigpen. Before the woman with the issue of blood was healed, she had to take the first step and touch Jesus. Before you get to your shifting season, you must get up and move.

This text is about leprous men who decided to do something to change their situation. They said, "Why sit we here and die?" As you study the surrounding text, you will find that these men decided to enter the camp. They felt they had nothing to lose. If they stayed where they were, they would die. If they went into the city, which was against the law, they would die. Like them, we must come to the place where we realize we have nothing to lose. We can sit and die or we can move forward and possibly die, but one way or another, it is time for a shift. It is time to move! When the lepers got to the camp, they found it abandoned with all the good stuff still in place. They helped themselves to food, drink, and silver. Listen, you have to move!

God operates in seasons and times, and one thing you do not want to do is miss your season or time. Ecclesiastes 3:1 tells us, "To everything there is a season, and a time to every purpose under the heaven." I do not want to miss my shifting season. I do not know how long it will be before it comes around again. And with seasons, timing is everything. You have to move when God says to move or you are going to miss it. You do not have time to stop and get everyone's opinion. You do not have time to wait for the prophet to show up and prophesy to you. You have to hear the voice of God and move when He says move. You can stand around or march in place when God gives you your marching orders. Get up! Move!

The men's decision to move resulted in God causing a noise of raging chariots that made the Enemy flee. When they fled, they left everything in the camp. The lepers had a feast. There was so much left they had to hide what they had and return for more.

Today, I encourage you to move. Don't worry about a future you cannot control. Don't worry about the ill intentions of others in regard to your life. Make a shift. Move from that dead place you are living in to a place of abundance.

God will handle those who may seek to kill us spiritually. When the Enemy comes in like a flood, God will raise a standard against him. Praise God in all and despite all.

Reflection & Application Questions:

1. What could making a conscious decision to shift mean for you? What do you need to do to change your place, position, or direction, so you can experience a shift in your life?

2. Based on what you have read, what will you change, learn, or strengthen to ensure your shifting results in abundance?

Scripture for Further Encouragement and Study: Psalm 100

16

I Made the Cut!

And Samuel said unto Jesse, Are here all thy children? And he said, there remaineth yet the youngest, and, behold, he keepeth the sheep. And Samuel said unto Jesse, Send and fetch him: for we will not sit down till he come hither. And he sent, and brought him in. Now he was ruddy, and withal of a beautiful countenance, and goodly to look to. And the Lord said, Arise, anoint him: for this is he. Then Samuel took the horn of oil, and anointed him in the midst of his brethren: and the Spirit of the Lord came upon David from that day forward. So Samuel rose up, and went to Ramah.
(1 Samuel 16:11-13)

In sports, making the cut is a big deal. Many people try out but several do not make the team. Some make the team only to be cut later.

Today's devotional is a word of encouragement for someone who feels as if your time and season will never come. It is to encourage you that you are already anointed for what you shall do at the appropriate time and in the right season.

David was known as a guy after God's own heart. As a matter of fact, it was that very characteristic that allowed him to be the chosen vessel he was. I believe if you are a man or woman after God's own heart, you will make the cut.

David was merely a shepherd boy. Saul, who was the king at the time, took it upon himself to do something only the priest was supposed to do: make a sacrifice. God rejected Saul, and Samuel began to mourn over him. God asked Samuel how long he was going to mourn over Saul. He told Samuel He had rejected Saul. Moreover, God instructed Samuel to fill his horn with oil and go to Jesse because one of his sons would be the king. When Samuel got to Jesse, he sanctified him and brought him to the sacrifice.

Here is Samuel with Jesse and his seven sons. The first son had a great countenance and stature. Samuel thought surely, the Lord is with this one. But God said, "Do not look at his countenance because I have rejected him." Remember, man looks at the outward appearance, but God looks at the heart. Sons numbers 2, 3, and 4 passed through but God rejected them also. Jesse's six sons passed by and none of them were chosen. But Samuel knew the voice of the Lord and that God said one of Jesse's sons would be chosen as the king.

If you know the voice of God and what He has promised you, do not stop; do not quit; do not give up until you see what He said! It does not matter how many opportunities or people come through your life, if it does not match what God said, keep it moving! Samuel asked Jesse, "Are all your sons here?"

Jesse said, "The youngest is keeping the sheep." In other words, he was not even invited to the party.

And here comes David. The Bible describes him as ruddy. *Webster's Dictionary* defines the word "ruddy" as having a reddish color. In my mind, he probably had a tan because he was a shepherd working outside all the time. The Bible also says he had a beautiful countenance and was goodly to look upon. In other words, David was not bad on the eyes. But this is not why he was chosen! Remember a few verses up God said He does not look on the outward appearance but the heart. God said to Samuel, "Arise and anoint him, for this is He." Samuel took the horn of oil and anointed David in the presence of his brothers.

Be encouraged that even though you were not invited to the party, you are the one who made the cut! You may not look like much to others, but you are chosen. Others may not think much of you and will not even invite you to be a part of certain circles or cliques, but you are the one God had in mind to do His will and His work here on the earth.

EncourageMe-N-It

You are God's choice; you made the cut! You know, some may not like the fact they were not chosen but you were. To make matters worse, they must stand by and watch the oil flow on you. Some are satisfied if you are in the field keeping the sheep. They can handle you being a shepherd but not a king. Do not let that bother you because your goal is to please God, not man. Rest knowing you made the cut. And like the oil flowed on David, the oil will flow on you both now and forevermore.

Reflection & Application Questions:

1. Have you ever experienced a time when God called you to do something, but you questioned if He really wanted you?

2. Did you do what He asked?

3. Based on what you have read, what will you change, learn, or strengthen to ensure you believe in yourself as God does and be obedient to His voice?

Scriptures for Further Encouragement: Philippians 1:6, Romans 8:30

17

A Necessary Sacrifice

"For unto you it is given in the behalf of Christ, not only to believe on him, but also to suffer for his sake"
(Philippians 1:20).

The word "necessary" is defined as absolutely needed, required. The word "sacrifice" is defined as an act of offering to a deity, something precious.

It was absolutely necessary for Jesus as something precious to offer Himself to God. So why was it necessary? "And almost all things are by the law purged with blood; and without shedding of blood is no remission" (Hebrews 9.22). Without this needed sacrifice, there would be no forgiveness of sins. Without the forgiveness of sins, we would not have access to eternal life. "For God so loved the world that He gave his only begotten son that whosoever believeth in him shall not perish but have everlasting life" (John 3:16).

Jesus became the sacrifice in our place. He died in our place. He died for us. Some say He was born to die.

We have already established that the shedding of Jesus' blood gave us forgiveness, redemption, and eternal life. Everything Christ suffered at Calvary gave us access to something powerful. "But he was wounded for our transgressions, he was bruised for our iniquities: the chastisement of our peace was upon him; and with his stripes we are healed" (Isaiah 53:5).

Jesus endured the suffering, and we reaped its benefits. We have access to forgiveness, peace, and healing. What a wonderful and awesome God we serve! Not that we were deserving because all have sinned and fallen short of His glory. "All we like sheep have gone astray; we have turned everyone to his own way; and the LORD hath laid on him the iniquity of us all" (Isaiah 53:6).

All of us are sinners. All of us were guilty and deserve death, but God laid our iniquities on Jesus, and He died in our place. Jesus was the propitiation for our sins: and not for ours only, but also for *the sins of* the whole world (1 John 2:2).

Everyone in the world has access to forgiveness and eternal life. No one has to die in sin make and hell their home. No one! We have restoration through the death of Jesus Christ.

And now we no longer live to sin, but we live in righteousness. Peter tells us that Jesus bore our sins in His body, so we can die to sin and live in righteousness; for by His wounds we were healed. Galatians 3:13 teaches us, "Christ hath redeemed us from the curse of the law, being made a curse for us: for it is written, cursed is every one that hangeth on a tree." Jesus carried our iniquities. He provided redemption, peace, and healing, gave us access, and became a curse for us!

With all this in mind, we have a part to play. We have a necessary response to a necessary sacrifice. What is our necessary response to a necessary sacrifice? What is absolutely needed or required from us in response to the precious gift of Jesus' death?

I am so glad you asked. Our necessary response to a necessary sacrifice is to receive Christ as our Lord and Savior. You simply follow Romans 10:9: "That if thou shalt confess with thy mouth the Lord Jesus, and shalt believe in thine heart that God hath raised him from the dead, thou shalt be saved."

Reflection & Application Questions:

1. How does it make you feel to know Jesus was the ultimate sacrifice for your sins?

2. Based on what you have read, what will you change, learn, or strengthen to ensure you respond appropriately to Christ's necessary sacrifice?

Scriptures for Further Encouragement: Hebrews 10:5-6, Romans 5:6-10

18

Pig Pen Revival

"And when he came to himself, he said, how many hired servants of my father's have bread enough to spare, and I perish with hunger! I will arise and go to my father, and will say unto him, Father, I have sinned against heaven, and before thee, and am no more worthy to be called thy son: make me as one of thy hired servants"
(Luke 15:17-19).

I have heard the parable of the prodigal son preached over and over again. Yet, every time, I hear something different.

In this story, the Prodigal asked his father to give him all his inheritance so that he could take his leave. The father did so, and the son went on his way. He went to a far country and wasted his substance on riotous (out of control) living. He was having a ball. I can imagine he was buying drinks for everyone and just showing off.

The Bible declares that when this young man had spent all he had, there arose a famine in that land. The young man found himself in want. And because he had no money, he had to go out and get a job. He joined himself to a citizen of that country. His job was to feed the swine. He went from being adorned in the best robes, having jewelry, and nice sandals to pouring leftovers into a slop for the pigs to eat. I am sure he wondered how in the world he got to that place.

The Enemy blinds the minds of haughty, prideful people. They mistakenly believe what they have, they will always have. I am sure this young man did not set out to fail in life. I am sure he wanted to breathe a little and have a little fun. But the s of having fun will not last!

Stripped of his former life and belly hungry, the Prodigal was face-to-face with what seemed to be his future. But then something clicked in his mind just as he was about to eat the leftovers that belonged to the pigs. He remembered how good his father's servants had it. At this time, he had a pigpen revival. Oh, what measures the Father will go through to get our attention.

Even in the pigpen, there are lessons to be learned. Do not despise the pigpen. The pigpen is the place where you come to yourself. The pigpen is where you realize you are more than what you have become. The pigpen is where you remember your Father.

EncourageMe-N-It

The pigpen is like a revival. You have an opportunity to come to life—to have your soul refreshed and revived. The pigpen is where you have that ah-ha moment and understand your need for revival.

Once this realization comes, the only thing left to do is to get up and go home. The father is waiting with a hug, not a hammer. The father is waiting to restore you—to dress you in your former attire. You show up at home ready to be a servant—but why be a servant when you can be a son?

When the world and life have beaten you down and taken everything from you, the only answer is to get up and go home. It is time to get out of that old attire. If any man be in Christ, he is a new creature. Old things are dead and behold all things are become new (2 Corinthians 5:17). The attire you wear now represents where you have been. The father's attire represents where you are going. I will not put on the servants' attire. I will put on the son's attire!

If you find yourself in the pigpen of your life, remember from whence you have fallen. Repent. Get up! And go home. At home, restoration awaits. At home, a new robe awaits. At home, new sandals await. At home, a feast awaits. You have a Father waiting with His arms open wide. God is anticipating, expecting, hoping, and watching for you to come on home. God and heaven are ready to rejoice over your repentance.

If you have tried to do things your own way, and it did not work out, get up and go home. God, your Father, is faithful and just. He will forgive you of all your sins. God is ready, willing, and able to clean you up and revive you. You are still part of His family. You still have an inheritance. You are still loved. Assume your rightful position as a son.

Reflection & Application Questions:

1. Where are you in your life right now? Are you in the pigpen, on the way to the pigpen, or have you experienced your pigpen revival?

2. Based on what you have read, what will you change, learn, or strengthen to ensure that wherever you may be in your life, someone is anticipating, expecting, hoping, and watching for you to come back home?

Scriptures for Further Encouragement: Romans 10:9, Psalm 51:12

19

RSVP for the Marriage Supper of the Lamb

"And he saith unto me, Write, Blessed are they which are called unto the marriage supper of the Lamb. And he saith unto me, these are the true sayings of God"
(Revelation 19:9).

Can you imagine the sound that will go forth once we leave this place and get in the physical presence of God? After all this time waiting for Him to return, finally, you will see Him face to face.

I do not think the praise will be nonchalant. I believe it will be loud and joyous just like the scripture said.

R—Get *real* about where you stand with God

S—*Salvation* required

V—*Value* your salvation by protecting it at all cost

P—*Prepare* for the supper

EncourageMe-N-It

Just as we wash ourselves every morning, we must ask God to wash and prepare us for His coming.

> *Not everyone that saith unto me, Lord, Lord, shall enter into the kingdom of heaven; but he that doeth the will of my Father which is in heaven. Many will say to me in that day, Lord, Lord, have we not prophesied in thy name? and in thy name have cast out devils? and in thy name done many wonderful works? And then will I profess unto them, I never knew you: depart from me, ye that work iniquity.* (Matthew 7:21-23)

> *Who shall ascend into the hill of the LORD? or who shall stand in his holy place? He that hath clean hands, and a pure heart; who hath not lifted up his soul unto vanity, nor sworn deceitfully. He shall receive the blessing from the LORD, and righteousness from the God of his.* (Psalm 24:3-5)

Make sure you have RSVP'd for the supper. Be certain you have your ticket. Once you do, the only thing left is to attend. We have all endured much in this life. In all of our going through and coming out, I am happy to know my

Natoshia D. Mayer

eyes have not seen or ears heard what the Lord has prepared for me.

We have been through the storm and rain but we have made it thus far. The operative word there is "been." This word is significant because it expresses a completed action. We are not *in* the storm. We have endured much pain, but we have made it thus far. The Enemy has tried to destroy us, but we made it thus far by the grace of God. Therefore, the Enemy has lost again. All that he tried only worked together for our good.

We endured because we held on. We have our tickets in our hands. Our reservation has been made for heaven. We have our RSVP in. Now we are bound for a city whose builder and maker is God. He promised to prepare a place for us, and one of these old mornings—and it will not be long—people will look for us, but we will be gone. As the song says, "We are going up to heaven to sing and shout, and there will be nobody able to put us out. They tell me there are streets of gold and gates of pearl."

Our loved ones have gone on before us in heaven. We will get to see them again. But, I want to see the man who died for me on Calvary. The One who set me free.

I want to see the man who picked me up, turned me around, and placed my feet on solid ground. I want to see my Lord and Savior, Jesus the Christ, Son of the Living God!

EncourageMe-N-It

Over in glory, we will rest from all of our labor. There will be no more dying or sickness. Jesus will wipe away all the tears from our eyes. We cannot let anyone or anything keep us from putting in our RSVP!

Reflection & Application Questions:

1. Have you put in your RSVP?

2. Based on what you have read, what will you change, learn, or strengthen to ensure you keep your RSVP and be ready when Christ returns?

Scriptures for Further Encouragement: Revelation 22:12

20

The Promise, the Instructions, the Manifestation

"And it shall come to pass, that when they make a long blast with the ram's horn, and when ye hear the sound of the trumpet, all the people shall shout with a great shout; and the wall of the city shall fall down flat, and the people shall ascend up every man straight before him"
(Joshua 6:5).

In this text, Jericho was closed up because the citizens were afraid of the children of Israel. The Lord told Joshua He had given Jericho into His hands. God gave Joshua specific instructions. Notice, God said he had "given," past tense, meaning it was already done. The purpose was already formed. However, it had not yet been manifested. Catch this, the thing standing between already done and manifestation is instructions!

God instructed Joshua to compass the city with the men of war once a day for six days. He said the priests are to have trumpets. On the seventh, the men are to compass the city seven times and then the priests are to blow with the trumpets. God even gave instructions on how the priests should blow. He said they should make a long blast with the ram's horn. When all the people hear the sound of the trumpet, they should shout with a great shout and the walls would fall flat. Afterward, the men of war would go up and take the city.

Joshua was armed with specific instructions. And being the servant he was, he was going to follow God's instructions explicitly. God knows how to handle your most fierce and experienced opponent. When going up against such an enemy, it is crucial to follow God's instructions. Because when your enemy is at his fiercest, he is still no match for God.

Once the instructions were followed, Joshua commanded the priests to blow their horns. The horns were the signal to shout! For six days, the people could not shout, they could not make noise. But now that manifestation was about to occur, it required a sound. Joshua said unto the people, "Shout! For the Lord has given you the city!" The trumpet blew and the people shouted with loud voices. As God said, the wall fell flat!

Today, I encourage you to let out a sound so loud every wall surrounding your blessings, increase, breakthrough, healing, and most importantly, your promise will fall flat.

EncourageMe-N-It

Whatever your wall may be, giving God a sound of praise can make it fall. There were no missiles, no hitting the wall with swords, no chipping away at the wall with knives. Obedience and persistent faith knocked the wall down.

If you feel your walls are not falling, stop and wait for God's instructions. Wait for the fullness of the Word of God and His instructions. After all, part of a plane will not fly. Part of a ship will not sail. Part of a car will not drive. All these things must be complete before doing what they were designed to do. You must be complete so you can do what God has assigned you to do on the earth.

With your instructions, you have your marching orders. The only thing left to do is what the Lord told you to do, how He told you to do it and for as long as He told you to do it. Then and only then will you receive the manifestation of the promise. For the promises of God are yes and amen!

Reflection & Application Questions:

1. Do you remember a time in your life when you moved on partial instructions? How did that end for you?

2. Based on what you have read, what will you change, learn, or strengthen to ensure you follow God's instructions to get all He has promised you?

Scriptures for Further Encouragement: I Samuel 15:22, Exodus 23:22

21

Who Is It?

"Lift up your heads, O ye gates; and be ye lift up, ye everlasting doors; and the King of glory shall come in. Who is this King of glory? The Lord strong and mighty, the Lord mighty in battle. Lift up your heads, O ye gates; even lift them up, ye everlasting doors; and the King of glory shall come in. Who is this King of glory? The Lord of hosts, he is the King of glory. Selah"
(Psalm 24:7-10).

When people come to our house and knock on our door, the first thing we ask is, "Who is it?" Depending on the response, the door is then opened or not opened. Today, the question is who is the King of Glory?

When you think about describing or defining the greatness or awesomeness of God, no single scripture can be read to accomplish that task. There is really no single word in the English dictionary that can describe God in all of His essence. To describe God is to describe *who* He is, not only *what* He does.

Some people know us by what we do more than who we are. We must constantly remind people of the difference between what we do and who we are. The older generation says God is a way maker; He is a lawyer in a courtroom, a doctor in the sick room. They say He is God all by Himself, and He does not need any help.

Who is the King of Glory? Who is the King of Glory to you? Only you can answer that question. Who keeps you even when you do not want to be kept? Who gives you peace in the midst of the storm? Who saved your soul and made you whole? Who picked you up, turned you around, and placed your feet on solid ground? Who encourages your heart in times of testing and tribulation? Who supplies all your needs according to His riches in glory?

We can agree that He is the King of Glory. He is the Lord strong and mighty. He is the Lord mighty in battle. If we only know Him by what He does, we are missing an important aspect of God.

Jesus is standing knocking on the door of your heart. Don't say, "Who is it?" You know Him. Instead, do what it takes for Him to come in. The scripture tells us:

> *Lift up your heads, O you gates! And be ye*
> *Lift up, ye everlasting doors!*
> *And the King of glory shall come in.*

Who is this King of glory?
The Lord strong and mighty, the Lord mighty in battle
Lift up your heads O ye gates; even lift them up, ye everlasting doors; and the King of Glory shall come in. Who is this King of glory?
The LORD of hosts,
He is the King of glory. Selah
(Psalm 24:7-10)

Reflection & Application Questions:

1. Have you ever been guilty of describing Jesus in terms of what He does versus who He is?

2. Based on what you have read, what will you change, learn, or strengthen to ensure you know *who* Jesus is as much as *what* Jesus can do?

Scriptures for Further Encouragement and Study: John 1:1, John 14:6

22

Where Is Your Faith?

"And Jesus answering saith unto them, Have faith in God" (Mark 11:22-23).

The preceding text tells us who to have faith in. Our faith must be in the right person. It is one thing to have faith in man, but it is a whole other thing to have faith in God. Doubt cannot remove mountains. *"For verily I say unto you, That whosoever shall say unto this mountain, Be thou removed, and be thou cast into the sea; and shall not doubt in his heart, but shall believe that those things which he saith shall come to pass; he shall have whatsoever he saith"* (Mark 11:23).

This verse teaches us we must open our mouths and speak. We have to speak to the mountains disguised as obstacles in our lives. This text also teaches us that doubt cannot move mountains. It is easy to *say* you believe, but do you really believe in your heart? God weighs the matters of the heart more than the words of the mouth. Our actions cannot *show* one thing while our mouths *say* something different. Our words and actions must line up.

We must know beyond a shadow of doubt that we trust God and place our faith in Him alone. "God is not a man, that he should lie; neither the son of man, that he should repent: hath he said, and shall he not do it? or hath he spoken, and shall he not make it good?" (Numbers 23:19).

If God said it, He will do it. When He does it is up to Him. Our job is to believe. If we speak and do not doubt but believe, the result will be moved mountains. If your mountain is not moving, increase your faith to at least mustard seed level. We increase our faith by hearing the Word of God (Romans 10:17). Also, check to see if you have placed your faith in something other than God. Only God can do what needs to be done in our lives.

You believe God can, but do you believe He will? More importantly, do you believe He will do it for you? Doubt is a tormentor. Doubt causes stress, anxiety, and depression. It causes mind battles. If you find yourself in the place of doubt—get out— and get out quickly. Whatever it takes for you to leave that place, do it. Say to yourself, "I can't reside in doubt and fear if I want to be a mountain mover!"

Whatever your mountain is, whatever that obstacle is in your life that seems too big to get over or get around, open your mouth and speak to it. It is up to you what happens to the mountain. It is up to you to climb or to speak. The choice is yours, which will you choose? Are you going to climb or speak?

Your level of faith determines your level of breakthrough. Little faith, little breakthrough, great faith, great breakthrough! Miraculous faith, miraculous breakthrough! Where is your faith?

Reflection & Application Questions:

1. Have you ever placed your faith in something or someone other than God? What was the result of that misplaced faith?

2. Based on what you have read, what will you change, learn, or strengthen to ensure your faith is always at a level where you can become a mountain mover?

Scriptures for Further Encouragement: Hebrews Chapter 11, Matthew 21:22, Romans 10:17

23

Birthing Promise

"For I know the thoughts that I think toward you, saith the LORD, thoughts of peace, and not of evil, to give you an expected end"
(Jeremiah 29:11).

Going through a birthing season is necessary for every child of God! In the birthing season, you will experience sickness because what you are carrying is growing and stretching inside of you. It will cause a feeling of unbalance.

You will feel as if you are not as close to God as you once were and for some, that will be true. There is nothing like pain and going through trials that get folks to stop pursuing God and start questioning Him.

You cannot think about the promise because the pain is so great. You cannot think about the fact that the pain is temporary because it is so raw, fresh, and real. But something is growing inside you. Something is being developed inside of you. And every single day, something new is developing.

Your promise is making its way to full term. While it does, you must adjust. You must change your eating habits and eat healthier. The Word of God is food. Eat it! Man shall not live by bread alone. Sometimes the Word is bitter and other times it is sweet. But the more you eat it, the more you give nourishment to your baby.

Inevitably, times of discomfort are ahead. The time will come when you are tired of carrying the load, no matter how excited you are. Before you get too tired, make sure everything is in place for the birth of your promise. Some of us have been expecting for more than nine months. Some of us have been waiting for the promise for a long time. What you do while you wait determines how easy the birthing process will be. If you just lay around during your carrying season, your labor will be harder.

But if you get up, move, exercise, and take care of yourself, the birthing process will be easier. If you read and study, you will know what to expect and be ready for it. If you listen to wise counsel, those who have been where you are, and gone through what you are going through, it will be easier. When I was pregnant, some of the best advice I got from my mom was not to tense up with the contractions but relax my body. It was hard at first because the contractions were very painful, but I

EncourageMe-N-It

eventually learned to relax my body and breathe through it.

Contractions are beneficial for pushing the baby forward. Spiritual contractions are useful for pushing your promise forward. Contractions for you could be your children acting up, your job shutting down, having your heartbroken, and feeling abandoned, alone, as if nobody understands. Those could be the very things that birth your promise. Be not weary in well-doing, in due season, you shall reap if you faint not.

There is an expected end. The expected end of a pregnancy is birth. The spiritual expected end is a promise. The only one who can push out promise is the one carrying it. Hence, you cannot quit now. You cannot give up now! Your promise is ready to come forth. Just as there is a due date in pregnancy, a due date is in place for birthing your promise.

Some of us are getting ready to move from a laboring season to a reaping season. You have carried the promise long enough. You have experienced enough morning sickness. You have endured enough swelling and being off balance. Your body and mind have gone through many adjustments. The only thing left is to birth your promise. Your promise has been cultivated in pain. Your promise has been cultivated through pressure. But now, the water has broken, and it is time to push! I cannot lie to you; it is going to hurt. But you must push.

Natoshia D. Mayer

The promise cannot stay in you past its time. If it stays in too long, it will be detrimental to your health Therefore, it is necessary to push! I know you are tired—but push! I know it hurts—but push! I know you want to stop because it is taking so long—but push! I know it seems it will take you out—but push! And when you feel you cannot push anymore—keep on pushing. And when it feels you are going to faint—it is okay. God gives power to the faint and to those who have no might He increases strength. Keep on pushing.

You have people around telling you to push. They are holding your hand and wiping your forehead. This is the last stage of expectancy and your promise is about to be birthed—push! The wait is over.

The phrase, "from labor to reward" is often associated with death. Today, we associate it with life. We have gone through labor for this promise and the reward is a manifestation and fulfillment of the promise.

Whatever dream or vision God has given you, it will come to pass in due season. No matter how far away it seems, there is an expected end. Though the vision tarries, wait for it—for it shall surely come to pass. Do not faint in labor—your reward is coming. The promise is coming. We have been carrying some overdue promises; they are past their due date. Are you ready to push those out? Do you feel if something does not happen soon, it could be detrimental to your spiritual health? God is a promise keeper. He gives us the victory and causes us to overcome. Nothing is too hard for Him!

We need the energy to push. How do you push? You push by lifting your hands in surrender to God. You push by casting all your cares on Him, for He cares for you. You push by taking your faith to another level. You push by taking your mind to another level. And whatever it takes, you need to be all in.

Do not give up during the press. Do not give up in the heat. Whatever it takes, be all in—mind, body, and soul. Hang on when times are rough and hard. Hang on when you cannot find the rope to hold on to, when the Devil is messing and shooting one arrow after another. Be confident of this very thing that He which hath begun a great work in you will perform it until the day of Jesus. It may not look like it to you, but He is working in you, so keep pushing out the promise.

Reflection & Application Questions:

1. What have you labored for in life and as a result received a great reward?

2. Based on what you have read, what will you change, learn, or strengthen to ensure you respond appropriately to operate in God's timing?

Scriptures for Further Encouragement: 2 Corinthians 1:20, Psalm 84:11

24

Three Strikes, You Are In!

"The woman then left her waterpot, and went her way into the city, and saith to the men, come see a man, which told me all things that ever I did: is not this the Christ?"
(John 4:28-29).

This text contains the story of a Samaritan woman. This woman came to Jacob's well in the heat of the all alone. Most women came early in the morning to avoid the heat. However, because of her reputation, she came in the heat of the day. On this day, when she came for water, Jesus was sitting on the well.

I would like to relate this story to baseball. All of us at some point in our lives have played the game of baseball. In this game, you have three strikes and then you are out. But today, I want to pull from this story and share how three strikes can mean you are in.

This woman had three strikes against her. The first was the fact that she was a woman. In biblical times, women were not regarded as much. In addition, women were not talked to in public, not even by their husbands. Strike two, she was a Samaritan. Jews and Samaritans have no dealings with each other. Samaritans were half breeds: half-Jew and half Samaritan. They worshipped idol gods. Jews worshipped the true and living God. So, there was tension between the two sects. The final strike was this woman's questionable reputation. Reading the text, you will find she had five husbands and the one she was with was not hers.

Although she had three strikes, she was not out. Before He made this particular trip, Jesus said He had to go through Samaria. He came to Samaria for this woman. She was counted worthy of a visit from the Messiah.

Sometimes if we are not careful, we will measure our worthiness by man's standards. If we continue to do so, we will never get anywhere. We will continue to strike out. If we wait for validation from another person, we will continue to strike out. If we stay stuck in the past, we will continue to strike out. But Jesus came to the well for you just as you are. Jesus did not bring up this woman's sins until after she asked for the living water.

We will not get some things in life until we ask for them. Ask and it shall be given. You have not because you ask not. Jesus told her if she knew who it was asking her for a drink, she would ask for a drink of living water. After further dialogue, Jesus said those who drink of the well will thirst again, but the water He gives will be a well of water springing up into everlasting life. Her response to Jesus was, "Give me this water, so I will not be thirsty or have to come to this well again." Then Jesus dealt with her situation. He asked her to get her husband. Of course, she said she did not have one. Jesus then told her she spoke the truth because she had five and her current husband was not hers.

She had never met Jesus and wondered how He knew her business. She perceived He was a prophet. Interestingly, this woman was not offended that Jesus knew her business. Actually, she was intrigued and continued the conversation. Afterward, she was so excited that she left her water pots and ran into the city. She told the people to come see a man who told her everything she had ever done. She said, "Is this not the Christ?" She did not miss her blessing by being offended.

The good news is it does not matter if you are at strike three. If God wants to change your life, you are not out; you are in! We have all had strikes and hit foul balls in life. We have even made it from first base to second base to third base only to have another batter strike out and cause us to miss our chance of coming home. But today, be encouraged. It does not matter if you have three strikes; you are in!

What are you in? You are in a new life in Christ. You are in for a blessing and a miracle. So much so you will drop your water pots and run saying, "Come see a man!" This woman was ashamed to even go to the well in the morning when the other women were there. I am sure people would point at her and whisper about her. So she waited until the hottest point of the day to come to the well. And when she came to the well, there was a Well sitting on the well. All this man wanted to do was give her life! Jesus did not care that she was a woman. He did not care that she was a Samaritan, and He did not care that she had a questionable reputation. He still offered her the living water.

Our past may be questionable, but our future does not have to be questionable. Come see a man! Do not let yesterday's sins keep you from today's blessings. Do not let yesterday's mess up keep you from today's miracle. Have a drink from the fountain that never runs dry. Get that living water that brings life. Jesus came that we may have life and have it more abundantly.

You may feel what you have done in life has given you three strikes but think again. Not only think again, believe again, hope again. There is life in Christ after the strikes. Whether you are on your first, second, or third, you are not about to be struck out. Know that three strikes make you in with Christ. Jesus hit a home run with the bases loaded with you and me. That means we are all able to come home. Jesus did not come to condemn the world but to give us life. Drop your pots today. Drop your past. Come running to the living water. Do not worry about the strikes you make in life. If you accept the living water, you are in!

Reflection & Application Questions:

1. What do you feel your three strikes are? What do you think has discounted you from being worthy to receive living water?

2. Based on what you have read, what will you change, learn, or strengthen to limit the Enemy's access, and strengthen yours to and from God?

Scriptures for Further Encouragement: John 7:37-39

25

You Took My Coat, But God Gave Me a Kingdom

And they took Joseph's coat, and killed a kid of the goats, and dipped the coat in the blood; And they sent the coat of many colours, and they brought it to their father; and said, This have we found: know now whether it be thy son's coat or no
(Genesis 37:31-32).

The story of Joseph is a very familiar story in the Bible. Joseph was given a special coat by his father which represented favor. The coat was precious in Joseph's sight as was Joseph in his father's sight. In relating the coat to favor, we have been given favor from our Father in heaven that cannot be taken away. Someone may have taken something from you that you really loved. Something that was important and identified your favor with man. The reality is all that anyone can take from you is your coat. The favor you have with God remains because it is not limited to any materialistic item.

Joseph's jealous brothers took his coat, but that action had no impact on the favor he had with his father. More importantly, Joseph's favor with God was not impacted. God had a kingdom that He was going to put Joseph over.

People may take your job, house, car, seat in the church, but no one can take your favor with God. What God gives no man can take away. We cannot worry about what is being taken from us. We cannot worry about what we are seemingly losing in this season. Doing so is being worried about the coat. It is worrying about what people can take. Instead, we are to focus on favor.

Joseph was sold into slavery, went down to Egypt, and later found himself in jail. However, even in jail Joseph had favor. Even though he did not have the coat, he did not lose the favor. This further reiterates favor is not in things but in God.

The magnitude of the test determines the magnitude of the miracle. Joseph had a rough test but what God was doing was taking Joseph from the field to the palace. The way from the field to the palace is paved with trouble and suffering. Sometimes it is paved with false accusations from others, losing friends, and even family. Nothing that paves the way stops the favor. Opinions and talk cannot take away favor. Do not get stuck in that place because it will keep you from getting to the kingdom.

While you are in your "through" season, use your gift to get you through the test. Your gift does not stop operating because you are in a test. Shift your focus from where you are to where you are going. Where you are is temporary. Joseph's dreams were not prison, his dreams were rulership. Therefore, he had to endure where he was to get to where God destined him to be.

I encourage you today, do not stop until your reality matches your God-ordained dream. Never let your mind land on victim but victor. Even from a place of confinement, you can still operate in the Kingdom. The questions we must ask ourselves is, can we still operate in the Kingdom without our coat? Can we operate without the pats on the back or the applause? Do we need the coat to prove our favor?

Yes, we can! No matter how long it takes you to get where your dream will be manifested, hang on in there because you will see the favor of God operating in your life. You will see the favor of God in you making provision for those around you. Like Joseph, people will survive because of you! You prepared in the pit and the prison! Now you have been promoted. You are ready to inherit the Kingdom. And not only are you ready to receive the Kingdom, you will ensure those who were the cause of the pit and prison still have provision. You can have the coat, give me the Kingdom.

Reflection & Application Questions:

1. Why is it dangerous to gauge God's favor based on materialism?

2. Based on what you have read, what will you change, learn, or strengthen to continue to keep your focus on seeking God's Kingdom and not man's favor?

Scriptures for Further Encouragement and Study: Mark 5:25-34, Psalm 9:10, Psalm 13:5

26

Course Shift Ahead

I will go before thee, and make the crooked places straight: I will break in pieces the gates of brass, and cut in sunder the bars of iron
(Isaiah 45:2).

In viewing life as a course, it is imperative that it is navigated well. Shifts in life are inevitable. However, shifts are manageable when we invite God to help shift our course. Course is defined as the act or action of moving in a path from point to point. Shift means to change place position or direction of. There are three things a course shift requires. Those three things are: movement, patience, and trust.

First, a shift requires movement. The course that is ahead of us may not always be in a straight line. It depends on the destination. If you have ever watched a train go through town and you were stuck behind the railroad crossing beam, you have probably noticed that the train stopped. The engineer had to pull a lever on the tracks to shift the direction of the train. So, a shift requires movement as the definition indicates.

A train is not like a car. It can only move forward and backwards. It cannot make a three-point turn. So, it is in the best interest of the train engineer to wait until the course has shifted to prevent going backwards. If the engineer moves forward too far, it will miss its destination and have to go backwards. In our spiritual walk, we can only go in two directions, forward or backwards. In order for a course to be shifted, a movement in place, position, and direction is necessary.

Secondly, a shift also requires being patient in the wait. While we are sitting behind those poles aggravated, it is the engineer's job to make sure the train reaches its destination. Can you be honest and say you have gotten aggravated in the wait? Can you go a step further and say you have tried to find an alternative course because of the wait? How many times have we been waiting on the beam to rise when we began to see people make U-turns because the train is just sitting there? And because the train is not moving people turn around and take the long way around as a result of impatience.

Our destination could be right on the other side of the tracts, but because of impatience, because we take matters in our own hands, it changed the course of our travel because we took the long way around. Impatience causes us to take the long way around. When it seems like God is taking too long to move, we get impatient, take matters into our own hands, make a U-turn, and go the long way around. A course shift requires patience.

Thirdly, we must trust the engineer. Do we think the engineer does not know that his stopping of the train will cause some people to have to wait? But the difference between us and the engineer is that he does not mind making you wait for his will to be accomplished.

To get the course shift we desire, we must understand the train is not moving until someone pulls the lever to shift the direction of the train to its intended position to reach its intended destination. We all have an intentional place, position, and intentional destination. What are we doing while we are waiting on the engineer to raise the beam? We could seek God to find out what to do so when the beam does come up, we will be ready to continue our course.

God is our spiritual engineer. He knows the course ahead. He knows when to release the lever and raise the beam. It is in our best interest as His children to trust God as engineer. We do not want to go backwards in life, only forward. God has promised to make our crooked places straight. Therefore, trust God as engineer to control the course and go forward only and not backwards. If we move too fast, we will miss the shift. We do not want to have to backup because we did not wait for the shifting of the tracks.

The engineer does not need your help. The engineer designed the course and will get you from point to point. He knows the location of every curve and every lever. He has been riding the rails a long time. He knows the course; He knows the path. The King of Glory is your engineer. Jesus knows your end from the beginning. Therefore, it requires trust on your part that He will make the course shift appropriately for you. God will make the crooked places straight.

Reflection & Application Questions:

1. What represents the train in your life? What is seemingly stopping you or blocking you from forward progress?

2. Based on what you have read, what will you change, learn, or strengthen to continue to trust God as your engineer and exercise patience in the course of life?

Scriptures for Further Encouragement and Study: James 1:4-8; Jeremiah 29:11

27

Hold On, Help Is on the Way!

"But ye shall receive power, after that the Holy Ghost is come upon you: and ye shall be witnesses unto me both in Jerusalem, and in all Judaea, and in Samaria, and unto the uttermost part of the earth"
(Acts 1:8).

Right before Jesus ascended into heaven, He told the disciples to go and wait for the promised gift of the Holy Ghost. Sometimes our only instructions are to get to a place and wait. Jesus declared when the power was coming in Acts 1:8: "And ye shall have power after." The key word is "after." Some focus on power, but power does not come until after. "After" implies something comes before.

You will not walk at some levels until after. After what? After you wait in expectancy and anticipate. In Acts Chapter 1, they waited. In Acts Chapter 2, they were endowed.

Some of us are in Acts Chapter 1 of our lives. We have the promise but we are waiting for the power. We know what God said, but we await the manifestation! Do not faint in the first act because the second act is on the way. Hold on. Help is on the way!

If you are like me, you have heard the promise. You have heard the prophecy. You have believed the Word of the Lord. However, the problem comes with the wait. Often, we are anxious when we have to wait. We want to know when something will happen, especially when we receive confirmation of a word spoken to us back to back from different people. We get frustrated and do not want to hear the prophecy anymore because it seems it will never come to pass. But do not give up! Acts 2 is coming!

I am sure the disciples had no idea the extent they were about to be used by God after receiving the promise. But God knew. He knew for them to do those mighty acts, they were going to need His power. They could not do it in their own strength. The assignment was too great.

We are not equipped or endowed with the power to do some of what we want to do yet. It can happen. God can do it but not yet. You have to wait for the appointed time. Those in the upper room waited for ten days. All 120 people in one room, in one accord waiting, anticipating, and expecting. I am sure they did not know what form the Holy Ghost would come in. They did not know if He would be in human form like Jesus or what. In spite of this,

EncourageMe-N-It

they held on to the promise until they experienced the power.

So, what do you do in the meantime? You do like the folks in the upper room. You hold on to the *promise* until you experience the *power*! The Bible tells us we will have power after the Holy Ghost comes on us (Acts 1:8). That was the promise! In Acts Chapter 2 when Pentecost arrived, the promise was manifested. This manifestation was the power!

First comes the promise then comes the power—in that order.

Trust God's timing. You have been obedient. You have been patient. You have waited. You believed the promise. Now, wait for the power you need to get the job done. You need the Holy Ghost to give you the power.

In the Old Testament Pentecost, the law was received. But on the day of Pentecost in the New Testament, the Spirit of Grace was received! (*Enduring Word Bible Commentary*)

I know it has been hard. I know the serpents have been busy. The scorpions have been stinging. But hold on! Help is on the way. As a matter of fact, let me change that to say

Hold on! Help is already here.

If you feel you have not gotten what God promised yet, go back, and wait for the promise. Do not move off the promise. The power is coming to the promise, so if you move from the promise, you may miss the power.

Reflection & Application Questions:

1. Can you remember a time in your life when you knew God had promised you something, but you had trouble waiting patiently for the promise to be fulfilled?

2. Did you get weary waiting?

3. Based on what you have read, what will you change, learn, or strengthen to reaffirm God's timing is not our timing and delay does not mean denial?

Scriptures for Further Encouragement and Study: Psalm 46:1-2, 10-11

28

Your Position Makes All Things Possible!

"And Simon answering said unto him, Master, we have toiled all the night, and have taken nothing: nevertheless at thy word I will let down the net. And when they had this done, they inclosed a great multitude of fishes: and their net brake"

(Luke 5:5-6).

Position – an act of placing or arranging.

In this text, Jesus is preparing the disciples for proper placement or position, so they may experience the overflow of fish. Reluctant and full of excuses, the disciples finally launched out and experienced the overflow. Overflow and blessings are at the end of obedience, even if you must change your position to experience them. The time is now to thrust out a little. Launch out into the deep. Position yourself at obedience.

When it comes to overflow, you need a word, proper position, and action. You must do something. So much can happen after a word from the Lord is given. Even surrounding conditions change at the word of the Lord. The conditions in this text were not right for such a great amount of fish to be present. If you know anything about fishing, and I do not, you will know too much noise scares fish away. You would also know that it is best to fish at night or early in the morning.

When your condition or situation does not seem ripe for a miracle, at God's word everything around you repositions and gets ready to overflow. Wherever God is, provision is. Peter went back out at the word of God, not necessarily his faith.

It is possible as soon as Jesus hit the water, fish started coming in His direction. I do not know. All I know is there were no fish—then there was an abundance of fish.

When they moved at Jesus' word and were in the proper position, they experienced the overflow. It has to be in that order. Overflow is not coming to out-of-position folks. Overflow is not coming to folks who do not move at God's word. It does not work like that. As I said earlier, provision is wherever God is. Therefore, you must get where God is to get what God has. You must go where He says go to experience the overflow.

Overflow is not coming because you are cute. Overflow is not coming because you know Bible verses. Overflow is not coming because of your title. Overflow is coming at the word of God!

I do not know about you, but I want the overflow. I want so much that my nets break, and I have to call someone to get in on this overflow. I want more than enough, so I can share with others, not just for myself.

To get there, you have to move. When you move your mind, the body will follow. Then and only then can you cast my nets out and catch so much you have to call someone to share the catch with. Your heart, mind, money, and time must all adjust because your position will make it possible.

Some of us are so far behind we cannot walk into our destinies; we must run! We must run like Forrest Gump. This time, you are going forth in a different position. This time, you know what works and what does not. The last time, it was on you. This time, it is on God. This time, your faith has been shifted to a better position. I know where my provision lies. I know who my provider is. His name is Jehovah Jireh, my provider.

He is better than a cable or cell phone provider; sometimes, their signals go out in a storm. But even in a storm, we can get to our provider, God. The line is always clear, and He never drops a call. If you have not experienced this, then maybe you need to switch providers. Come on over to the One whose seeds have never been forsaken or had to beg for bread. Switch providers!

Make up your mind this time, it is going to be different. What will make this time different? Your position shifted. At God's word, you moved. At His word, you are lowering your nets again. Even though you tried so many times in vain, you will try again. You may say like Peter, "Lord, we have worked hard all night and did not catch anything!" You have worked on something so many times and ended up with nothing. You have quit or put it on the back burner. Nevertheless, at His word, you will try again. You will live again. You have re-positioned yourself, cast out your nets, now, it's time to pull up and pull in.

Your overflow will be so great your nets will break. Now that's overflow!

Reflection & Application Questions:

1. Have you ever been out of position with God and as a result, you missed what He had for you?

2. Based on what you have read, what will you change, learn, or strengthen to remain in the position to receive the overflow?

Scriptures for Further Encouragement and Study: Philippians 4:19, I John 5:14

29

You Have Your Instructions, Now Go Win the Battle

"And when they began to sing and to praise, the LORD set ambushments against the children of Ammon, Moab, and mount Seir, which were come against Judah; and they were smitten"
(2 Chronicles 20:22).

When facing obstacles larger than yourself, the answer to overcoming is in your praise. The answer also lies in following the instructions of the Lord. When you obey God and praise Him in all things, He will handle what is larger than you.

The initial response for Jehoshaphat when the children of Moab, Ammon, and others came against him to do battle was to fear. Often times, our reactions to overwhelming situations are also fear. But Jehoshaphat did not stop at fear. He sought the Lord and proclaimed a fast (2 Chronicles 20:3). In response to seeking the Lord and fasting, the Spirit of the Lord came upon Jahaziel. The Lord instructed him not to be afraid or dismayed because of the size of the multitude. He told them that the battle was not theirs but God's. He went on to tell Judah that they needed not to fight in the battle but stand still and see God's salvation. Most importantly, He let them know the Lord was with them. Jehoshaphat appointed singers to go before the army. The Bible says when they began to sing, the Lord set ambushments against those who rose up against Judah, and they were smitten.

We glean from this story that whenever we face giant obstacles, whenever it seems there are more against us than for us, we need to use our instructions. Our instructions have been given in the Word of God. Once, we have them, we are to praise God because He fights for us. We have no need to fight in this battle.

Once you put aside your fears, the Lord will ambush the thing desiring to take you out. And your praise will confuse the Enemy. When you have every reason and right to turn around, don't do it! Hang on in there and remain faithful. It confuses the Enemy. When you seek God for instructions, instead of assuming the worst, it confuses the Enemy. In all your ways acknowledge God and He will direct your path.

The fighting in some areas of your life is over. Notice I did not say the fight is over. There will always be a fight between good and evil. The only difference is as God's child, you do not have to fight some battles. Your fight in battles is on an as-needed basis determined by God. Let us not fight in battles that were never designed for us. In some battles, you shall hold your peace and allow the Lord to fight for you.

Other battles require you to set, stand, and see. *Set* yourself in seeking God. This means to get positioned and postured. Then, *stand* still for instructions. Finally, *see* the salvation of the Lord. Get ready, set, win! God knows your enemies' positions and plans. Hence, He will place you where you are sure to win. You have your instructions, now go and win the battle!

Reflection & Application Questions:

1. Can you remember a time when you were facing something so overwhelming that fear set in? How did you handle it? What do you wish you had done differently?

2. Based on what you have read, what will you change, learn, or strengthen to be sure you are always listening to God for instructions and to know when He wants to fight on your behalf?

Scriptures for Further Encouragement and Study: Exodus 4:14, Deuteronomy 3:22, 20:4, 17

30

Press in, Pass By, and Touch

"When she had heard of Jesus, came in the press behind, and touched his garment. For she said, If I may touch but his clothes, I shall be whole. And straightway the fountain of her blood was dried up; and she felt in her body that she was healed of that plague"
(Mark 5:27-29).

The familiar story of the woman with the issue of blood provides great insight into perseverance and faith. This woman had been dealing with an issue for 12 long years. She had spent all she had to get better, but she actually grew worse. Having spent all she had and seeing doctors who could not help probably left her in a desperate state.

One day, she heard about Jesus. From what she heard, He was her answer. Faith comes by hearing. She had not seen what Jesus could do yet, but something in her connected with what she heard, and she believed if she could only touch Him, she would be healed. She said, "If I can just touch." She did not want to wait for a touch from the Lord; she decided to do the touching. However, touching Jesus would require pressing and passing by the crowd.

How many times in our lives have we said, "if I can only"? If I can only get over this or stop that. If I can just get out of debt or over this sickness. Today, I encourage you to understand that the answer to "if I can just" lies in the press, the pass, and the touch. You have to press past the thoughts that try to keep you bound. Press past the crowd that is standing between you and the touch. And then you have to spiritually touch the hem to be made whole.

Do not miss the blessing in touching Jesus' clothes and not His body. Everything connected to Jesus carries what He carries. Do not miss that—everything that touches Jesus, He touches. The robe was touching Jesus. The woman said, "If I can touch what is touching Him. I do not need Him to lay hands on me. I do not need Him to even speak to me in front of all these folks. I do not want to be noticed; I want to be healed." Who can honestly say, "I don't want to be noticed; I want to be healed"? Check your faith.

It was faith that reached out and touched the hem. Immediately, the bleeding stopped. Have you ever been in a season where you just wanted the bleeding to stop? You just wanted the pain to go away. You were tired of going through the same thing year after year—nothing changing, nothing getting better.

If you have, then the answer is to press in. How do you press in? Get up and do something! Make up your mind to get your touch. And you do not care how many folks are around Jesus, you will press past the folks.

Everybody in the crowd did not need what this woman needed. Everyone in the crowd may not have been as desperate as she was. Everyone in your circle may not need what you need. Their issues may not be yours. They may not be as desperate as you are. So make up your mind to press and touch.

You may have to say to some, "I'm sorry; I don't mean you any harm, but I have to get to Jesus." You may have to elbow pass some. You may have to step on toes. Say, "Please excuse me, but there is a touch I have to make." When you make that touch, it will immediately stop the bleeding. It will instantly resolve your issues. This touch is different from any you have ever received. It will make you whole, deliver you from all of your issues, and change your life. This touch will get Jesus' attention.

When this woman touched Jesus, He knew He had been touched by someone who needed help. He felt the virtue leave Him (one version said He felt power leave Him). One touch causes healing virtue and power to be released. Jesus turned and said, "Who touched Me?" He is God. He knew. Jesus never misses a teaching moment. His disciples were confused. They said, "With such a great crowd, how can You ask who touched You?" Testimony time—in seeking not to be noticed, she was noticed. She came forth afraid. Everyone heard her tell what was going on with her. Jesus' response was, "Daughter, thy faith hath made thee whole; go in peace and be whole of thy plague." She went from "Woman" to "Daughter."

I encourage you today, whatever is plaguing you, the answer is in the press, the pass by, and the touch. If you are desperate to be free, freedom awaits you in the touch. This woman felt in her body the issue was gone.

That can be your testimony. One touch can change your life. Faith yields results! You have to want it bad enough. The song says, "When you have tried everything, and everything has failed, try Jesus." But I say try Jesus before you try anything else. If you do that, you will not have to try everything or anything else.

Trust God and touch Him with your issue. Jesus is not here physically so the way to touch Him is with your faith. Believe one touch will change your life. Regardless of how long you have been dealing with whatever you are dealing with, there is enough power in Jesus Christ to heal everywhere you hurt. He is able. There is nothing too hard for God. He is a healer! He is a deliverer! He is a Savior! He is God! But you have to press in, pass by, and touch Him.

Reflection & Application Questions:

1. Do you remember a time you were dealing with issues that seemed as if they would never end? How long was it before you sought the Lord for help with that issue? What was the result of getting help?

2. Based on what you have read, what will you change, learn, or strengthen to use your faith to touch Jesus?

Scriptures for Further Encouragement and Study: **Mark 5:25-34, Psalm 9:10, Psalm 13:5**

Made in the USA
Columbia, SC
21 November 2020